SWALLOWING YOUR PRIDE
AND OTHER ENGLISH EXPRESSIONS

by Andrew Niccol *pictures by* Stephen Woodman

SPHERE BOOKS LIMITED
London and Sydney

First published in Great Britain by
Sphere Books Ltd 1984
30-32 Gray's Inn Rd,
London WC1X 8JL
Copyright © 1984 by Andrew Niccol
Cartoons copyright © 1984 by Stephen Woodman

TRADE
MARK

This book is sold subject to the condition that
it shall not, by way of trade or otherwise, be lent,
re-sold, hired out or otherwise circulated without
the publisher's prior consent in any form of
binding or cover other than that in which it is
published and without a similar condition
including this condition being imposed on the
subsequent purchaser

Reproduced, printed and bound in Great Britain by
Hazell Watson & Viney Ltd, Aylesbury, Bucks.

Catching the measles.

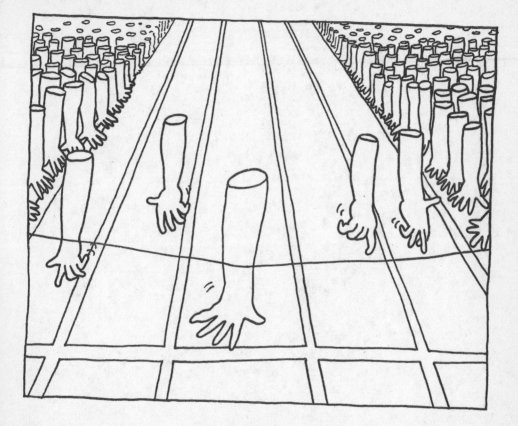

The arms race.

A one-night stand.

Making a Charlie of yourself.

Breaking wind.

Jumping to conclusions.

A heart attack.

Taking a liberty.

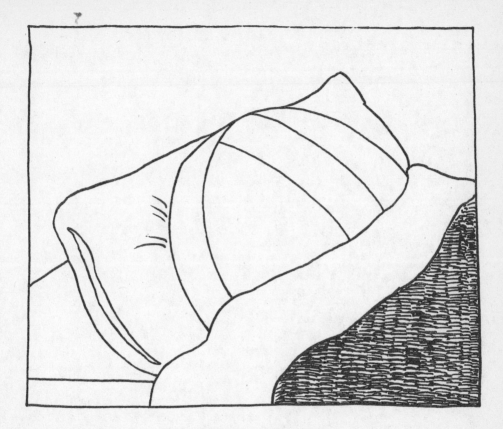

A sleeping pill.

Having a brush with the law.

Bringing up the rear.

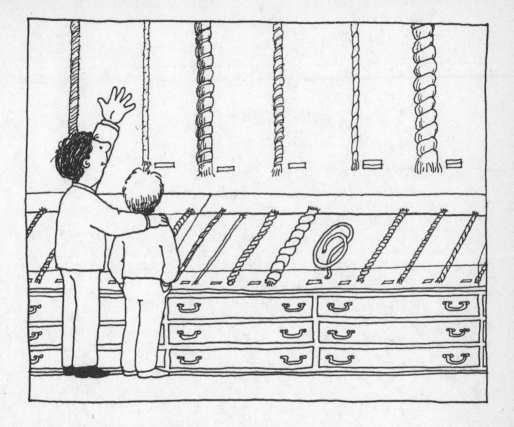

Showing someone the ropes.

Dope smuggling.

Tit for tat.

A topless waitress.

Going out on a date.

Feeling sick.

Putting someone's mind at rest.

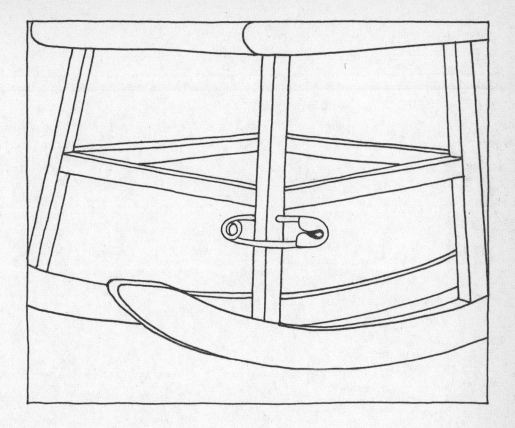

A punk rocker.

Shaking hands.

Giving someone the creeps.

Striking while the iron's hot.

The vice squad.

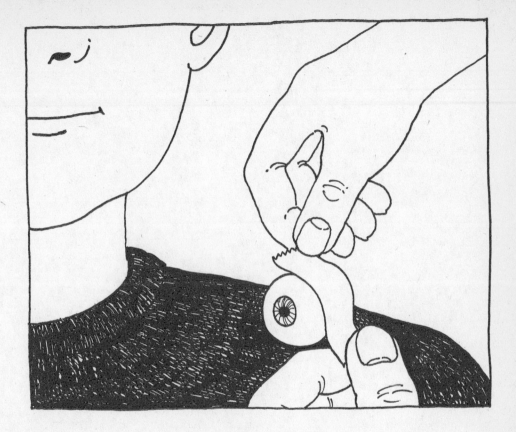

Keeping an eye on someone.

Doing odd jobs around the house.

Calling someone a taxi.

Playing hard to get.

Making ends meet.

A working bee.

Shoplifting.

Swallowing your pride.

A training bra.

Having your nose in a book.

Leaving well alone.

Taking out the garbage.

A bad spell of weather.

Keeping a stiff upper lip.

Watching your step.

Getting cold feet.

An armchair critic.

Saving someone's bacon.

Changing your mind.

Having someone round for dinner.

A cop-out.

Starting a family.

Having the last word.